Give
Happiness
a
Chance

Photographs and Illustrations

Maria Bartha: 93
Jean Ber, Fotogram: 66–67
Camera Press: 69, 80
Mark Collins: 62
Susan Currant: 46
John Doidge: 52
Eric Evans: 10–11, 35, 37, 73, 95, 96, 108
Helen Exley: 85
Richard Exley: 18–19, 23, 24, 26, 51, 58, 61, 82, 99,
100–01, 103, 104–05, 106, 111, 112–13, 114, 119
Gianna Grazia: 6, 31, 64–65, 74, 78
S. O. Hakansson: 57
Thomas Höpker: 4
H. Hyatt: 87
Curt Ingemar: 8
Sylvester Jacobs: 43
Oswald Kettenberger: 32
Wolfgang Kunz: 88
Jean-Claude Lejeune: 116
Robert Lieberman: 122
Michigan Travel Commission: 120–21
National Park Service: 125
Norsk Press Service: 28–29
H. Armstrong Roberts: 55
Claire Schwob: 14, 49, 76
Frits Solvang: 41
Abisag Tüllmann: 17

Published 1980 in the United States of America
by Rand McNally & Company

© 1979 Exley Publications, Watford, England

Original edition Menslief ik hou van Je! © 1972 Uitgeverij Lannoo,
Tielt, Belgium

Also published in Afrikaans, Dutch, French, German, Italian,
Japanese, Norwegian, and Spanish

Printed in the United States of America
by Rand McNally & Company

Library of Congress Catalog Card Number: 79-91535

Give Happiness a Chance

by Phil Bosmans

Rand McNally & Company

Chicago • New York • San Francisco

By way of introduction

For years now
I've spoken to people on the 'phone.
Here now I've put
my thoughts down on paper.
I know only too well that one cannot always help
with a few soft words.
Still I've written them down,
because I was asked, nearly begged, for them.
In reality, I will always say the same things
to unknown, invisible callers.
Sad people. Troubled people.
People who want to learn to live again.
I'm like an absurd prophet
who sows his seed in the wind,
not even knowing where the field lies,
and always using the same seed—
seed he himself received from somewhere else.
In fact, I am just a funny little dwarf,
who kicks against the modern idols
of your foolish world,
and pursues you
at your well-filled table or buried in your newspaper,
watching your television or at work,
going about your business
and during every conversation,
with that awkward question about your 'heart'.

But one thing I know..
That a word that touches the heart,
changes the heart.
If you are tired,
and you don't know why,
then one word can be a happening,
a piece of bread before a new beginning,
hope for you when your life has become a desert.

Contents

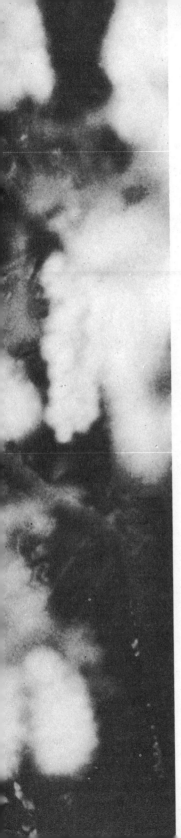

Hello there

Hello there friend.
Use your time to be happy.
You are a walking marvel.
You have no equal.
You are unique, irreplaceable.
Did you know that?
Why aren't you surprised?
Why aren't you glad, astonished
about yourself
and about everyone else
you know?
Do you think that it's so natural,
so obvious,
that you are alive,
that you can go on living,
that you are given time
to sing and to dance,
and to be happy?
Why then lose your time
in the senseless pursuit
of money and possessions?
Why make a crowd of worries
of tomorrow and the days after tomorrow?
Why quarrel, bore yourself?
Why drown yourself in empty amusements
and then sleep when the sun shines?
Take your time quietly
and be happy.

**Time is no speedway
between the cradle and the grave
but space
to find a place in the sun.**

Nothing is
without meaning

My eyes are for the light,
for the green of Spring and the white of the snow,
for the grey of the clouds
and for the blue of the sky,
for the stars at night,
and for the incredible miracle
of so many wonderful people around me.
My mouth is for the word,
for every gentle word
someone is waiting for.
My lips are for kissing
and my hands for softness, for tenderness,
for giving comfort and bread to the poor.
My feet are for the path
which leads me to the dispossessed.
My heart is for love, for warmth,
for those who are abandoned and left in the cold.
My body exists to be close to others.
Without my body I am nowhere.
Nothing is without meaning!
Everything has a deep significance!
Why then am I not happy?
Are my eyes closed?
Is my mouth full of bitterness?
Are my hands 'grabbers', and is my heart dry?
Don't I know
that I was born for joy?

Pills!
Pills!
Pills!

For the smallest pain, a painkiller.
Every night a sleeping pill.
And for gloomy thoughts
a couple of Valium to cheer you up.
You are hopelessly spoiled.
You turn everything into a problem.
The slightest difficulty
and your nerves go to pieces.
Problems have to be tackled.
The problems that you evade
will start to fester.
Yet, there are a whole heap of problems
which are just part of life—
    in marriage,
    in education,
    in growing up,
    in getting on with people,
    at work.
These are problems which you have to accept.
You have to go through them
without hesitation,
with courage and with strength.
If you run away from them
they will follow you and weigh you down.
In your life you can't ignore your cross
without being crushed by it.

The same thing, day after day

People are ill with boredom.
Weary of life.
The house is full.
The table is loaded with food.
There's never a 'new' day.
Everything stays the same, day after day.
The walls are thick, always cold.
New life never enters in.
People are ill with boredom.
They no longer even see the flowers or the birds.
Their parakeets and their overfed dogs
are as dead as they are.
People go out at night
till the early hours of the morning,
then sleep when the sun shines.
They go to the doctor,
to the psychiatrist.
They never feel really good.

The happy people

In searching for
the deepest reason for human happiness
I have never found the source
to be money, possessions, luxury,
lazyness, profiteering, party-going or excitement.
With happy people
I always found, deep down, a sense of security,
a great simplicity,
and a spontaneous joy in little things.
With happy people I was always surprised
by the absence of stupid desires.
With happy people I never found
restlessness or passionate searching,
never that lust for self-importance.
And most often they had a good dose of humor.

Whistling in the rain

How is it that some people
sit in the sun looking like sour apples
—and that others
whistle in the rain?
How is it that there are people
who, as soon as they open their eyes,
see *something* wrong?
It is because they don't understand
the meaning of life,
the meaning of things.
They need God,
not as an impersonal, hazy being
somewhere far away,
but as a personal friend,
like a father, close to them.
By being on intimate terms with God
people see things with new eyes,
and start every morning
with a new heart.

Is life sometimes too heavy for you?
Try for a while to be like a clown,
who weeps inside,
but laughingly
jokes and plays for a child,
to cure the sadness
in his own heart.

If you can't laugh,
you can't live

Laughing is healthy.
You need to laugh.
Humor is healthy.
Do you think enough about this aspect of your health?
If all your anxieties give you wrinkles in your heart,
you will soon have wrinkles on your face.
Laughing frees you.
Humor relaxes you.
A laugh can free you from needless intensity.
A laugh is the best cosmetic for your outside
and the best medicine for your insides.
If your laugh-muscles work regularly
your digestion will improve,
your appetite will be stimulated,
and your blood pressure will stay down.
Humor gives you a sense of proportion.
Laughter and fun don't only influence your metabolism,
but also your surroundings.
They lessen the tensions
and the tears.
Laughter and fun free you from that deadly earnestness
about leaden problems,
free you from that miserable daily drag.
Laughter and fun are the best remedies
for the drugging of your heart and mind.
Laughter and fun open out new spaces
for the still unknown joys of life.

A day when you don't laugh, is a lost day.

Trifles

Why do I look so ugly when I miss the bus?
Or can't borrow the car and have to walk for once?
Yet I know that in Asia people have to walk every day,
between the poles of a rich man's rickshaw
—for just a handful of rice.
Why do I grumble about a minor illness
and worry about wrinkles or spots
when I know that thousands
carry an incurable illness in their body.
And thousands are being tortured for their beliefs,
for the color of their skin or for nothing at all.
Why do I feel put out when I have to wait in line,
or walk in the rain or when I'm kept waiting?
Don't I ever think of others, those with no legs,
or those who must live in bed,
the people who would be so happy, *just once*,
to be able to stand in line, or, *just once*,
to walk in the rain, or to be kept waiting.
And if my meal isn't served on time
why do I forget that millions of people
are never able to sit at a full table?
We are laughable, pathetic, stupid creatures,
who spoil our own lives, who spoil the lives of others,
because of a multitude of petty trifles,
when we ought to be so grateful
for every new day, for all the good things of life,
which we don't even deserve.
We have a fever
and our fever is really a madman's selfishness.

A spoilt day

I will never be happy
if I have no control over my emotions,
if my day is spoilt
by a scratch on my car,
an angry word at home,
a mini-crisis at work,
an unkept appointment,
a less-than-perfect result,
a wrinkled stocking
or a crooked tie.
I will never be happy
if I am the victim of my own emotions,
a slave of my own desires,
a prisoner of overgrown expectations.

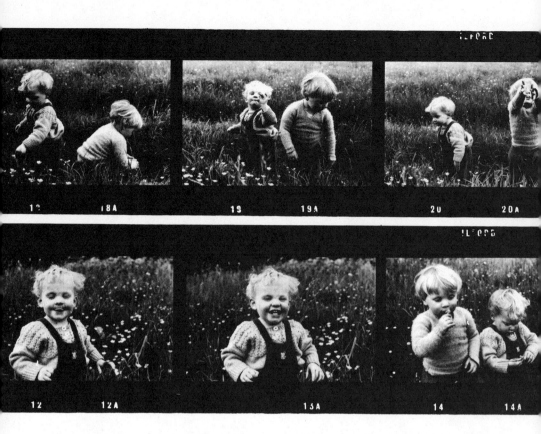

Where have the flowers gone?

Tell me.
Where have the flowers gone?
The flowers of delight in life,
the flowers of pretty and nice things
in the TV reports, the newspapers
and in daily conversation?
They died and suffocated under an avalanche of news
about hatred, violence, murder and petty scandals.
Nobody has seen the flowers.
Nobody has heard about them.
They died and suffocated in the wallets
of sensation-seekers
and on the lips of doom-prophets.

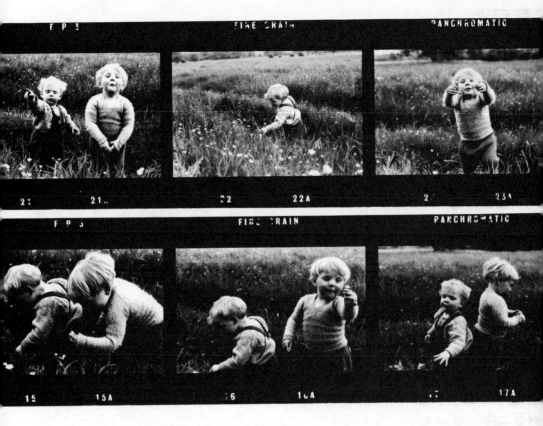

Tell me.
Where have the flowers gone?
The flowers of little things done for each other.
The flowers of being a gift for each other.
The husband for his wife.
The wife for her husband.
All people for each other.
They have died in our self-will,
suffocated in our so-ridiculous sensitivity,
in our mini household cold-wars.
Tell me.
Where have the flowers gone
of that tiny bit of happy security
we can offer each other?
You have a heart,
and there's a human being who needs you.
Bring on the flowers!

19

Call to the Spring. Meet the sun.
Let yourself be captured by the wonder of light
and of life.
Look at the skylark
who sings so high in the air.
Do you know why?
Because he doesn't have to pay any rent!
Look up at the sky and sing,
because the sun is free
and it shines for you.

Simple flowers will do

Why have so many people got nothing to live for?
Because they have no friendships.
Because they don't know anybody who likes them.
Because nowhere do they find
an ounce of sympathy and affection.
Because a flower never blooms for them.
And yet flowers work wonders!
No need for expensive or rare flowers.
Common simple flowers will do—
a smile, a kind word, a simple gesture.
The smallest tiniest flower
given with a warm heart
tells a lovely story.
A pure, sweet story about a small piece of
heaven-on-earth,
where the people seem like angels,
where, for every anxiety,
for every pain and for each tear,
there is a soft comfort,
where the people, like flowers, bloom for each other.

Park in the sun

In reality, I don't have such a long time on this world.
Between the eternity before my birth and the eternity
after my death, I am given such a short time for parking
on our little planet.
I have my own parking meter.
I can't put back its hand. Neither can I make it give me
more time by popping in a few more coins.
My parking time here is relentlessly limited. There is
not a single thing I can do about it. My life is like my
name written in the sand: a tiny breeze and it is gone.
So what should you do?
Don't whatever you do cry about it. Try to park your
life in the sun and not in a wasps' nest of quarrels and
wrangles, of nerve-wracking worries and problems.
Make beautiful days! Be enthusiastic about light, about
life, about good people and about good things. Be
friendly and warm to the old man who knows that his
parking time is nearly over. Be warm towards the sick,
the handicapped, the dispossessed, the disillusioned,
the cheated and the many unhappy folk who no longer
have a place in the sun. Make beautiful days for them
and for the people around you. You have to do
nothing more to be happy in yourself.
Park in the sun and let the parking meter tick.

A time for silence

The next time you have five minutes to spare, do you know what you should do? Just think!
Make sure that for once you are surrounded by silence. Switch off your radio and your hi-fi. Turn off the TV—and the lights. Shut your books, put down your papers and magazines. Flick the switches. Turn off the taps. Free yourself from the tentacles of our consumer society. Like a frightening octopus, it sucks away what remains of your freedom and spirit with its debasing commercials.
Make everything silent around you. Make it silent within you. And take your pulse. You must find out whether you're already dead—buried in goods, in that tight corset of money-making, buying, consuming, fashion-following, profit-making, achieving.
At a thousand meetings you talk, you protest. The poor of the third world, the poor at home—they will get nothing out of your talk, your arguing, your protests, your resolutions.
They loathe them because they know you yourself are drowning in the very things they *must* go without.
They will take you seriously only when your consumption-fever cools off. I do know something to take for this consumption-fever: it is restraint, self-denial, sacrifice!

The city

High rise after high rise.
Full of people.
So many name-plates,
nicely shining name-plates.
A lot of people,
well cared-for people,
people who don't know each other.
They see each other.
They stand together in the elevators.
They look straight ahead.
Each one knows that the other person is there,
just as they know that a pole exists,
which must not be bumped into.
People in the city.
People alone in the city.
The city is no longer
a likeable, cozy home
for people.

Nobody came

Barry fell dead in the street.
A crowd of inquisitive people gathered around him.
The traffic stopped.
The police picked him up
and deposited him at the morgue.
Three days in succession they waited for a relative,
a friend, an acquaintance to come.
Nobody came.
Then Barry was placed in a special refrigerator.
What a symbol.
A refrigerator for people who are forgotten.
They waited another two weeks.
Still nobody came.
Then one afternoon
he was put in a hearse
and taken to the cemetery—
buried like a lost object.
Barry
was a human being,
a man
alone in the city,
buried long ago
by other people.

People without faces, without hearts

Can I warn you
against the coldness
that has come over our world?
A coldness which has frozen so many people.
People live alone
in a dry desert of people,
like ants,
in shops and streets,
in trains and buses
and rented rooms.
People without faces,
without hearts.

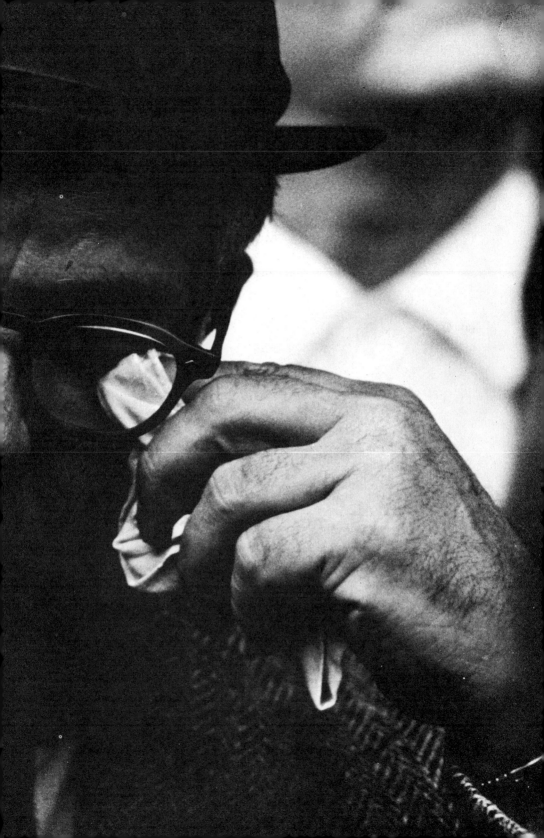

Because man follows
the rhythm of the sea

A human life is so wonderful, so unbelievable.
Year in year out,
day in day out, you move among people and things.
Some days the sun shines and you don't know why.
You are at peace.
You see only the warm and good sides of life.
You laugh, you dance, you give thanks.
Your work seems easy. You get on well with everyone.
You don't know why. Perhaps you are sleeping well . . .
Maybe you've found a close friend
or you have a sense of security . . .
You would like this time of calm and deep joy
to last forever.
But suddenly everything changes.
It is almost as if too bright a sun
has brought on the clouds.
A kind of indefinable sadness comes over you.
Everything seems black,
You think that no one likes you anymore.
Any trifling thing seems to give you a reason to complain,
to grumble, to be jealous or to reproach.
You think things will go on and on like this,
that this mood will never lift.
And once again you don't know why.
Perhaps you are tired.
You don't understand it. Why must it be this way?
Because a human being is a piece of 'nature',
interwoven with days of Spring and days of Autumn,
with the warmth of the Summer and the cold of Winter.
Because man follows the rhythm of the sea—
ebb and flow.
Because our existence is a continuous repetition
of 'living' and 'dying'.

If you grasp this, you can carry on,
with courage and trust.
for then you know in yourself that after every night
a new morning will come.
If you can accept this, you will be able to live through
the regular rhythm of 'up' and 'down',
more deeply, and with a sense of joy.

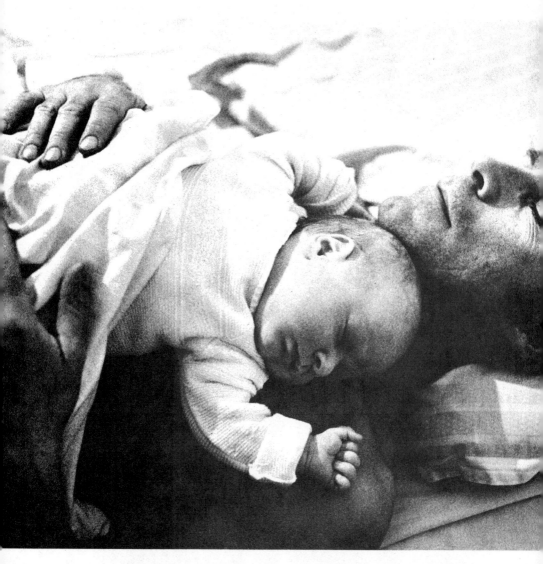

It's wonderful to be 'man', to be alive! To be an
ordinary person, to look at the sky, at the sun, at
the flowers and, in the evening, at the stars.
Watching children, laughing, playing, working,
hoping, loving, day-dreaming, being content. It
is a daily feast.

To be alive

To live simply and normally, to be good, not always wanting everything, not to be jealous, not to nag or complain, but to help, to do more, to comfort, to visit a sick person, to stand by if someone needs you, to make yourself tired for others, to fall off to sleep in a comfy chair, to eat and drink together . . . and all this not because you must or because it's important, but because it makes sense to you, because you are human, a fellow-man, because you're alive.

Do you know the danger that threatens you these days?

You live in the times of the 'useful'. "What purpose does it serve?" That's what people ask. "What use is it? Will it pay? People weigh up the cost, the efficiency and the end-product. People are busy. People are pre-occupied. People are weighed down. People calculate. Money must be the result. And people forget that the beauty of life is found in moments that are not calculated, when people are living very ordinarily, very simply. People live longer and longer but they are not happier and happier. They begin by working in order to live and they end up working and forgetting to live. They haven't grasped the essential thing in life. They still continue to believe that a person's happiness lies in possessing more, eating well and living longer. In these days of so much knowledge, how can people be so thick? Defend yourself. You are not a machine made for one particular purpose. You are more than your function, more than your profession, your trade, your work. You are first and foremost human, made to live, to laugh, to have love, simply to be a good person. And *that* is the only important thing in this world!

Pomposity!

In those opulent glass and concrete buildings, pompous men sit heavily in their seats. I see them sitting in dead earnest endlessly discussing their weighty and petty problems. The files pile up. They grow like some gigantic fungus. The cabinets fill up. The offices fill up. The whole world fills up, until it becomes completely dark! What do you think we can achieve with that kind of world?

Why don't people burst out
in fits of loud laughter
at large meetings,
or watching TV, or at important receptions,
when they see
how deadly serious some people are
as they build up their own importance
and struggle to keep up a façade.
Why don't people laugh
when they see
others who lose themselves in the labyrinth
of their own little vanities,
where in a pseudo-scientific way
and with a frightening earnestness
they devalue the real worth of life
and in its place
cultivate a narrow-minded selfishness?

Words are weapons

Take care when you speak in judgment.
Words are powerful weapons,
which can cause a lot of tragedies.
Never make a person look a fool with your tongue.
Never make a person look small with your big mouth.
A hard word, a sharp word,
can burn a long time,
deep in the heart, leaving a scar.

Accept that others are different,
think differently, act differently,
feel differently, speak differently.
Be mild and healing with your words.
Words should be 'lights'.
Words should calm, bring people together,
bring peace.
Where words are weapons,
people face each other like enemies.

Life is much too short,
and our world is much too tiny
to turn it into a battlefield.

"Lord help me
to keep my
big mouth shut,
until
I know what I want
to say.
Amen."

Talk is 'in'. Action is out

Talk is 'in'.
Action is 'out'.
Never has there been so much talk as there is today.
Never has such an avalanche of hollow,
pointless words crashed down on people's heads.
Everyone wants to talk.
Everyone wants to put in a word.
Everyone wants to interrupt.
But only a few have anything to say.
Because only a few can bear the silence
and effort needed to think.

Sad times

Sooner or later you bang your head
against the inevitable obstacle
that turns your life into a cross.
You become sick.
You have an accident.
Your loved-one dies.
Your career is a failure.
You are deceived, abandoned by your husband or wife.
Things go against you.
People pull you down.
You are humiliated, ruined.
You can't go on any more.
You grow old.

This obstacle can be any shape or size.
It doesn't take any notice of your degrees,
your standing, your name, your reputation,
the size of your wallet, your relationships
or your success with people.
You seem lucky.
Everything is going well . . .
Then suddenly that dark cloud looms up.
It can hurt you so badly, that,
disillusioned, disheartened and battered,
you'd rather be dead.

This tragedy, this obstacle,
is a reality in every person's life.
But fewer and fewer people can cope with it.
They can't accept it any more and become over-anxious.
Many go down under the strain.
Doctors and psychiatrists are overburdended.
You have no choice.
Either you bear your cross
or it will crush you.
But you cannot carry your cross,
unless you learn to understand its function.
The cross brings you back to truth,
to the reality of your vulnerability,
— your exact human size, your insignificance,
your poverty, your feebleness.
The cross can free you from material things,
which threaten to drown you.
You can cut free from your mediocrity.
The cross is like an aerial,
which can pick up a message from God.
It won't take away your pain,
but it will take away the senselessness,
the purposelessness of it all.
You can feel human again
and, perhaps, feel and see everything clearly,
through eyes that have wept.

Kiss your life

For the umpteenth time I've just seen a man suffer
shockingly from the irreparable loss of his wife.
Rebellious and irreconcilable, he made me think of
another man who once sat here before me, many
years ago. At first he looked like a block of granite, with
a vacant stare, a stone-hard mask for a face, with a
menacing expression. Between long silences, the
words which came from his mouth sounded just like
swear words, "It can't be. It mustn't be. My wife is
dead. Killed. I can't feel it. I'm going to kill myself . . .
I potter about, can't work, go through bottles of
sleeping pills. Nothing helps".
"Try to accept it", I say softly.
"I can't! I won't!" he blurts out, "I'm putting an
end to it."
Sometimes life treats people dreadfully.
Arthur Miller wrote in one of his plays: ". . . I had a
child and even in the dream I saw that the child was my
life; and it was an idiot. And I wept, and a hundred
times I ran away, but each time I came back, it had the
same dreadful face. Until I thought, if only I could kiss
it, whatever in it was my own, perhaps I could rest.
And I bent to its broken face, and it was horrible, but I
kissed it."
Yes, I believe that eventually you must take your life in
your arms—your life just as it is. Accept it, kiss it, no
matter how heavy or how hard it seems. If you've once
kissed it, it will be different, bearable.
But don't have any illusions. Happiness is no
'continuous performance'. Real happiness in life comes
and goes and usually doesn't last very long. The rest of
the time you dream of it and wait for it. Kiss your life.
Accept it, just as it is. Today. Now. So that those
moments of happiness you're waiting for don't pass
you by.

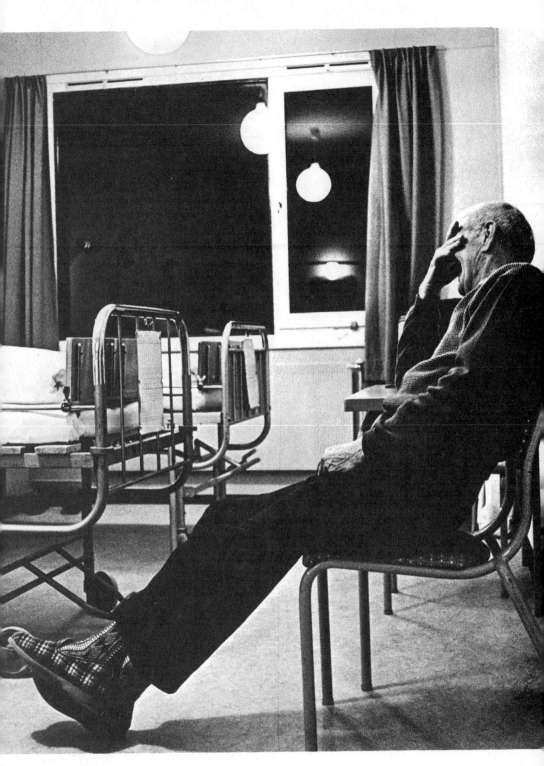

Personal concern

I must never imagine I've dealt with love
if I only feel 'friendly' towards the people around me.
This is woolly sympathy,
an illusion of friendship.
I put myself at ease.
I do nobody any harm.
I let everyone else get on with life.
Hold it!
If I am a perfect citizen,

well off and safe under my glass dome,
with my very own atmosphere,
that is exactly how I became an accomplice
to that collective indifference
which strangles our society.
If I really want to love
I must give myself fully to a deep and true concern
—above all for those few people
closest to me,
those who are entrusted to my care,
those people who share the same roof with me,
who work with me each day,
who travel with me,
who romp and play and laugh with me.
This kind of concern is binding and drags me away
from my own small protected little world.
This concern is essential if I am not to shrivel up.
I must never postpone it,
not even if it disturbs my peace and tranquillity.
Perhaps it does me good to be disturbed.
Perhaps it is good to be occupied
with acts of kindness to others,
and that this sometimes involves pain and sorrow.
And that some day
I may even have to carry the burden of anxiety
without being able to talk about it to other people.
Personal concern is the fruit of real love.
It may cause me to suffer,
but ultimately, it brings with it the best of all gifts.
It gives life.
It gives color to my existence,
and even, at odd moments,
an immense feeling of profound gratitude
—a foretaste of an unknown paradise.

In love again

Being in love is wonderful
just like Spring in your heart.
Everything is different.
Everything glows.
If you're in love
everything is pretty and sunny
because up to now
you've become half blind,
blinded by the depressing,
heavy view of life.
There are many sides to being in love.
But there is one kind of love
that we need more than ever before
in our complicated, problem-laden society,
in our society which has had an overdose of psychiatry.
It is being in love
with ordinary everyday things.
Recent discoveries
have not been discoveries of wisdom,
but discoveries of speed
that don't bring us one step
closer to happiness.
Discover again with me
the ordinary things,
the simple charm
of friendship,
a few flowers for a sick person,
an open door, a welcoming table,
eating plain old fish and french fries
or a hamburger,
lazing in a garden chair

gazing at the sky,
a handshake, a grin,
the quiet of a church,
a child's drawing,
the opening of a bud,
the chirping of a bird,
a row of poplars,
a stream, a mountain, a cow . . .
Life becomes a feast
if you can enjoy ordinary everyday things.
It is Spring! Yippee!
**I'm in love again
— with ordinary things.**

**Don't forget
that every day is given to you
as an eternity to be happy.**

Concentrate
on little things

I like the people around me.
I like joy, and this way joy comes back to me.
I like friendship, and this way my life is blessed,
and my days are full of smiles.
I don't have to possess a thing to enjoy it all.
There is so much to gain
if I concentrate on little things,
and on ordinary little people.
There are so many surprises
and so many wonders to be discovered.
In all things there is a memory of lost joy.
Being able to see this is the art of living.
I know it is not easy to get to heaven,
and I know, for sure, that it is impossible
if heaven has not come to me first.
Heaven must start on earth wherever people are friends
and where kindness is passed on with joy,
from hand to hand.
But, of course, every sky has its clouds.
I am not always in the best of moods
and friendships become like dried prunes.
Still, that is not a problem to feel sad about.
If friendships grow into dried prunes,
I pour some water on them and they swell again.
Life is a compulsive adventure, with God and people,
in a world of give and take.
I want to be neither a hero nor a martyr.
but a funny little man, who gathers the forgotten flowers
and laughs at the big people of this world
who sit on power and riches.
I like the people around me.
I like joy, and this way joy comes back to me.
I like friendship, and this way my life is blessed,
and my days are full of smiles.

Richer than the richest man

Don't weigh out your love like a grocer. Don't measure out in advance how much you will give, how far you will go in love. Be spontaneous in love. Carefully weighed and measured love is not love. It is calculation. That way you miss the joy. That way your love doesn't bring happiness. That way there may not actually be a war, but you live with indifference and each day passes you by like a tedious slow train. That way you will never feel warmth inside you, you will never feel like dancing and singing.

Spontaneous love is something fantastic; spontaneous love for your husband, your wife, your children, your father and mother, for a child lost in the street, for a person who suffers or for an outsider. Spontaneous love is a gift, which lifts you up to the highest level of human joy. But remember—it's not what you possess that brings abundance, it's the things you can enjoy. If you can enjoy a flower, a smile, the playing of a child, you are richer and happier than the richest rich man. He has everything he can dream of and still feels dissatisfied, incapable of enjoying things anymore because—like a rich man's donkey—he is trapped, held down by the weight of bags of treasure.

When I am thoroughly satiated, my eyes are glued shut and my heart stands still. On the highest step of consumption, of luxury and of wealth, I die as a 'human being'.

Lord, free me from my possessions, which possess me
and make me so very ill.
Free me from my pride which deforms me and makes
me so small.
Free me from my greed which misleads me and makes
me so ugly.

Lord, save me from that inner unspoken-of longing for
things that can never satisfy me, and which fire my
foolish hunger even more.

Luxuries
and possessions

You search for security.
You dream of living together with joy and happiness.
You want a relaxed life and a pleasant atmosphere.
And you begin to buy, and buy, and buy,
because you sometimes have more in your purse
than in your head and in your heart.
And you buy antique furniture
and smart furniture.
And you buy curtains
and downy carpets and solid floor tiles.
You want soft lights and reading lights
and a cozy corner
and a reading corner
and an eating nook.
By merely flicking a switch
you get everything you could want.
You have your own 'bar'
and you can fill your house with music.

POOR PROSPERITY'S CHILD.

Why then don't you look happy?
Why do you laugh so little?
And why do your nerves get on edge so quickly?
Why do all these luxuries finally leave you
so empty and so unsatisfied?
Because they are dead things.
Very practical perhaps and really remarkable.
Things that have a use,
but which you can never exchange
for one gram of love.
And it is love you need.
But you can never buy love.
If you pay for love,
it isn't love any more.

The computer forgets your heart

To be a human being, a good human being — that is the only important thing in the world. But who is interested in that?

Goodness includes simplicity, caring for others willingly, and a large dose of self-sacrifice. But who still acts that way? These things are completely out of fashion, no longer to anyone's taste.

Here and there one hears demands for a new deal, a new world. But one seldom hears about these important basic ingredients. That's why the statements about restructuring society and developing the community are so much hot air. People don't believe it all any more, because there's no sign of it in their daily lives.

The outside world only has eyes for big things, conspicuous things, which alter the balance on the modern scale of values: career, reputation and money. You will not be asked about your goodness, your simplicity, your kindness — but about your school results, your university degree, your ambition, your scientific and technical skills. People are looking for the technical or scientific person who fits into an opening, as far as possible avoiding the subject of feelings like pity, understanding, caring for others or time given to those in need. This is the danger that threatens us in

this over-organized and bureaucratic society.
The computer doesn't take your heart into
consideration.
Otherwise, how could so much abominable suffering
still exist in our world? The good people are powerless.
The power and decisions lie with the world's
anonymous leaders, who still behave as though
everything on earth is their private property.
Be a good person, through and through. Then that
small piece of earth where you live and work will be a
better little place.

Two plus two equals five

Man is not a machine. He is not a cog in a wheel. He can't be fitted into inflexible equations. Two plus two equals four. That's fine for mathematics, but it won't do for human beings.

The best person scores only 1 out of 10, or 2 out of 10 for his life. But even if he achieves less, I wouldn't be surprised, and certainly would not judge him. I would admire him if he had done his best, whatever the result. In this day of computers and electronic apparatus, man runs the risk of being reduced to a robot, which can be accurately maneuvered and executes to perfection the directions it receives.

If society endangers people, they must save each other. Be fully human, profoundly happy to have another person, even if it is someone with broken wings.

Why?

"I had just taken him a cup of tea in bed," says the woman. "He felt so much better. When I came up again he was dead. But why? He was still so young."

Every day, every hour, there are people in villages and
cities, in busy high streets and quiet lanes, in enormous
hospitals and country clinics, in plush drawing-rooms
and pitiful bare rooms, or somewhere along the road—
people who in their deepest need cover their face with
their hands and cry out because of so much
inescapable sorrow, and who, helpless and
desperate, cry over a pitiless death.
Why so much suffering?
Why multiple sclerosis?
Why cancer?
Why so many handicaps?
Why an accident which means never again being
able to walk?
Why die in the Spring of life?
Why? Why? Why? Who or what can answer this
question for me? Science? It knows and will explain to
me in the tiniest detail the exact causes of my suffering
and my death. But what use is a scientific explanation
to me?
When I think of the dead and of my own death, and
the suffering of innocent people, I find myself
absolutely mystified. I can try not to think, to forget the
whole subject, to fool myself. But as long as I have any
brains and a heart, it will pursue me. When the hour
comes when I too must feel the darkness of suffering
and death, then nothing will be left for me *but* to
accept.
I hope that in that hour I will be able to pray, will be
able to shout to God: 'Why do you put out the candles
which you yourself lit?' And then I am sure that I will
learn with my heart all the things I can't understand
with my mind.
That God is love.
He loves me.
He holds me.
That I will die to live forever in love, which will not die.

Winter

Cemeteries full of white chrysanthemums.
Death dressed in white.
The dead and the living together for a moment in one
place. They seek each other, they think of each other,
unable to reach each other. There is, somewhere, a
frightening separation, a boundless helplessness.
Suddenly I think of my own death, and I become a little
frightened. The fear of death touches the joy of life.
Death is the most powerful spell breaker. It darkens all
feelings of light-heartedness, gnaws at every certainty,
and blocks my ability to breathe in the joy of my
existence.
Nobody knows how to give advice about death.
Neither does science.
People are silent, people forget. The traffic rushes on
again as soon as the funeral procession has passed.
But I must not banish all thoughts of death from my
consciousness. That is the politics of an ostrich. In the
end everything leads to this one basic question, "Is
death the end or isn't it?" If death is the end, my death
takes on the character of a frightening amputation. If it
is not the end, my death takes on an amazing,
awakening, new dimension. A restful meeting with
death, that critical moment in my life which I must go
through quite alone, places me either before the
fullness of all things, or before complete nothingness;
either before the meaning, or the complete
meaninglessness of my existence; either before God,
or the infinite void.
The secret of life and death is very near to the secret of
God. Just as my own unique, original 'I' does not find
a proper explanation in physics, chemistry or biology,
so I find no solution to the meaning of God by studying
natural sciences.
I hold in my hands just one single thing. It is hope. A
hope that gives me joy in life until my last breath.

In the big world, the business-like world,
of achieving men, of belligerent men,
mothers come last.

In this cultureless world of computers
and self-service, super-store style,
mothers don't count.

Mother's Day is a simple, happy time,
when children use their fresh young imagination
to prepare little celebrations for their mothers.
It is a living protest against the exploitation
and disfigurement of woman's image
in a society of super-abundance
and senseless mass culture.

We need women more than ever

Now that the highest values in life are under siege, we need women more than ever—outside the family too. We need them—married or single. Not to scream out at us from those life-size posters about their whiter-than-new wash, or their fresh-breath toothpaste, or their even-better-figure-hugging bra. No truly liberated woman will be exactly charmed to see her image widely projected as a cover-girl, pin-up or sex-object on display to all.

A woman has a much fuller, deeper, more important role. Her whole fertility, her emotional fertility, must be allowed to flower again. Women are vital in our man's world, which centers around technology, around manufacturing and buying, around hard-headed business, power and competition. Her mysterious, feminine humanity, her feeling for small everyday things, her softness and tenderness towards the frailty of all things, her sensitivity and her motherliness, make living and working together a joy.

Each woman has an immense, captivating task to do in this world, provided she herself has not had her spirit crushed in the wheels of a soul-destroying production machine. The role for tomorrow's woman will be decisive in reshaping our society from an inhospitable stopping-place for the weak and poor, into a home full of love for everyone.

Love from friendship—this love leads to light,
to peace and to deep joy.
This love never harms people.
It does not possess for itself.
It leaves the other person free.
And when it finds expression
in physical tenderness,
it stays pure.
But when one person wants
to possess another for himself alone,
for his own satisfaction,
he destroys the person he thinks he loves.
And destroys the friendship.
True, you will never be capable
of a totally unselfish friendship.
But you must always keep trying.

Love and friendship

I always ask myself why people can't stay in love.
Why is loving so difficult
for people who live together, day after day?
I am convinced that we often believe our own pretense.
We think that we love someone else.
But, in fact, we only love ourselves; we love 'me'.
Each one expects too much of the other.
It is the other person who must be pleasant.
The other person must build me up, must help me out,
must never be grumpy, must never nag.
At the slightest failing, I feel hurt.
We think too little, maybe never,
about what we ourselves can give
or can do for our partner.
Don't blurt out without thinking,
"You don't love me any more."
No, not before you yourself have given everything.

Living together,
day after day

People find it very difficult
to go on loving each other.
This is true for married couples.
After starting with an avalanche
of declarations of a love so deep
that you would gladly die for each other,
there comes the down-to-earth realization
that, after all, you are not
in the mood for dying for each other every day!

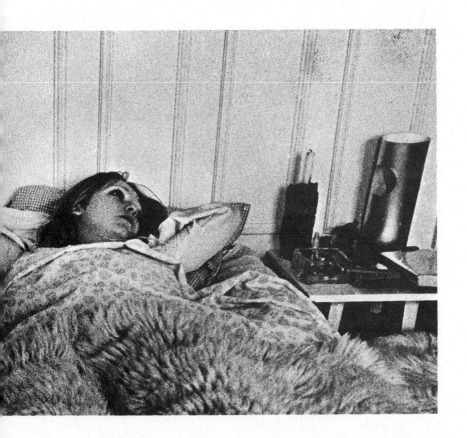

A beautiful gift

The most important thing I must give,
but the most difficult, is forgiveness.
Forgiveness. Yes, that is it.
I must forgive, always, again and again. Forgive.
As soon as I stop forgiving, I build a wall.
And a wall is the beginning of a prison.
Above all in life I've got to do two things
—understand and forget.
I know many people
and I know the secrets of many people.
And I know only too well
that no two people are the same.
Each person is an entire world in himself
and he lives and feels and thinks and responds
from his own world.
And the deepest core of that world
is still unknown to me.
Therefore it seems obvious that,
in the normal course of events,
disagreements, frictions and tensions will develop.
Only when a person understands
that other people are different,
and only when he is ready to forgive,
is it possible to live together.
Otherwise there is a state of mutual siege
and you live in a day-in, day-out,
cold or hot war.
There are many exceptionally good opportunities
for us to make peace,
or to make up quarrels.

We so often get a chance to give a small present,
to send a postcard inviting someone around
as a sign of reconciliation, of forgiveness.
Once the first step, the most difficult step, is taken,
the rest is easy.
Forgiveness. The most beautiful gift.

Love and sex

People are looking again
at the value of physical love.
A body is no donkey.
Nor should it be treated like a pampered doll.
We grow closer to each other through our bodies,
to meet in joy and friendship.
Without bodies we are lost.
And it is a good thing
that sexuality has been dragged
from its secret dark cell, into the open.
Sex can be a valuable positive force
which helps people to develop, to blossom.
But when it is repressed or twisted
its wonderful power
is distorted into restlessness, craving and anxiety.
Sexuality is not life's ambition
neither can it be life's fulfilment.
And by itself it offers no security.
The best human sexuality
unfolds and is meaningful
only in an atmosphere of real love,
where hands don't grab
but signal caring and tenderness,
where the body is brought alive,
freed from anxiety and craving greed.
It is a warm harbor,
a peaceful haven
and it offers deep security.

Absolute freedom in sex is loveless.
Even in marriage.
Because absolute freedom
is always the freedom of the strongest,
the jungle of the most brutish self,
where the wishes and feelings of another
are ignored.
Pornography is loveless,
because it ignores people,
because you don't find a mind or a heart there.
Just naked bodies,
in a cultureless, tasteless exhibition
of frustration and bare flesh.

Sex maniacs can't enjoy love
and that is exactly why they're insatiable
and sometimes aggressive and dangerous.
Just study the dreadful acts
and sex murders in the papers.

The concept of freedom

There is a lot of confusion about the concept of freedom. It exists amongst older folk as well as the young.

In the name of freedom there are men and women who are casual about faithfulness in marriage, there are children who totally ignore their parents, and the gutter press prints blatant lies. In the name of freedom people can do their own thing and turn their backs when someone needs help. People continue to live to suit *their* feelings, *their* likes, *their* whims. This is the freedom that is respected, even worshipped by the selfish. This freedom leads dead-straight towards the jungle, to the tyranny of the strongest, the most wily, the most brutal.

Freedom is only meaningful, valuable and joyful in a climate of love. Because it so happens, that in this world, what matters most is not freedom, but love.

A person who loves, forgets himself and gives others power over him, gives a slice of his freedom to others. Love sets a person free for the beautiful, the good, the true and for the deep joys of life.

Tower
of Babel

I am dismayed by people's awful inability to get on with each other, to understand each other, to love each other. Press, radio and TV dish up an almost deadly daily dose of war, violence, murder, brutality—it's a senseless show. Enough to suffocate us.

All these conferences, committees, protests, manifestos and debates don't seem to improve mutual understanding.

In his own way, everyone wants to work towards peace and a better world. But no one seems willing to forgive, to bury the hatchet. No one seems to be determined to change *himself*. Everyone wants to blame someone else. Everyone wants to accuse, attack or make someone else responsible. That way we are heading back towards the tower of Babel. We are possessed by the spirit of Babel—the feeling of confusion, contradiction and darkness.

Just for once, try to be quiet and calm. Give time to discovering the feeling of peace, of God, of love. If this feeling comes to your heart, you will also reap the rewards. They are fantastic rewards. They have these names: love, joy, patience, friendliness, kindness, faithfulness, comfort, gentleness and simplicity.

Civilization?

Hate and armaments surround us. The newspapers
scream out about murder, violence and scandals. And
we call ourselves civilized people, cultured people, real
humanitarians. And we call ourselves Christians, while
we are busy squashing out the awkward annoying
cross from that same Christianity. We no longer feel
like making an effort, a sacrifice.
We choose Christianity in an easy chair, with a warm
bed and a full larder. We camouflage our finely
developed conceit with superficial, cozy words.
Recently, in the suburbs of Paris, I met a poor Flemish
priest working among the needy. "In history," he said,
"we had a period of heroes and of will-power. After
that, the romantic period. In the nineteenth century,
the time of enlightenment and the intellect. Today, we
live in the culture of instincts. Yes, of the instincts:
money, sex, violence and consumption".

Jungle

When I come into contact with people and with human need, I often get the feeling that I'm in the jungle. I watch the way people are being crushed, sometimes in the friendliest possible way, simply flattened by a human steamroller.

Modern barbarians are often neatly-dressed gentlemen sitting behind shining desks. They push buttons and sign letters. They never dirty their hands. Their weapons are locked up in the safe. In the world of business and the world of finance there are merciless gangsters who make it their business to strangle the small and the weak.

In the world of the sick, of the old, of the disabled, in the world of people who once made mistakes, in the world of people who are unable to help themselves and who are totally dependent on others, there is a sort of monstrous exploitation. Weak people and people in distress are extra-vulnerable. This is why greed and love of money are even more horrible where these people are concerned. Isn't it inhuman to grow rich on the back of someone else's need? When I work among helpless people, love—not money—must come first. If my profession is to care for the sick, the old, the disabled or the suffering, I must, above all, understand and love them. Here, it is much more important to serve than to earn; anyone whose only interest is to make money out of need is guilty of one of the lowest forms of exploitation.

A haunting image

One evening,
during the TV news,
I was shocked by a picture,
a picture flashing between
the usual nightly scenes
of wars and calamities.
Just before the sports news
there was a picture that got in between
for just a second.
A picture from one of the richest
countries of the world,
with remarkable welfare services,
where, from cradle to grave,
everyone is cushioned.
A picture from Sweden.

    I saw an old man lying on the pavement.
    I saw people walking past him.
    The announcer said
    that this man had been lying there for hours,
    without anybody turning round to look at him.
    Finally, a police car came.
    The man was dead.

This picture haunts me.
It is a picture
from a dead, decadent civilization.
Did nobody see this man fall?
Why had nobody covered him up?
This is a public murder by indifference.
Or, to his fellowmen,
perhaps this man had already been dead
for a long time.

You know how small, how poor, how lonely, how
weak and how vulnerable people are. You know that
there are tears that nobody will ever care about. You
know that there is almost no sorrow greater than that of
a heart which nobody understands. You know that life
is an unbearable pain for some people.
Be gentle!
Do what you can to understand, to help people. Step
inside their grief, their desolation. Step down from the
heights of your self-sufficiency to the valley of the
people who are alone and who suffer; down to the
people out in the open who are without shelter and
without security.
Never be hard. Never judge them.
Be gentle and try to understand their inexpressible
longing for lost happiness, as well as their sometimes
silly hankerings and needs.
Then you'll be happy yourself.
Then, in your own loneliness and weakness, there will
come moments of serenity which will lift you right out
of the daily grind of life. You will have a heart big
enough to comfort everyone, to hold them all.
In gentleness lies never-ending comfort, for all people
who are left in the icy cold of our form-filling,
computerized society.

Loneliness

You can be alone without being lonely. You can be single and feel quite secure and happy. But you can be married, or even in the company of a thousand people and still feel horribly lonely.

Loneliness is a moral disease which can't be cured by crowding people together. More than ever people are crammed on top of each other in high rises, in busy streets, trains, supermarkets, cinemas, bingo halls and vacation resorts. And it's precisely in these places that the loneliness becomes sharper, still deeper.

This loneliness, which afflicts so many people today, grows from deep spiritual emptiness, from confusion, and from insecurity. Psychiatrists stand helpless before it and anyway, most people don't have enough money for psychiatric treatment. There can be some improvement, but very seldom a cure. The therapist has no power over the root causes of today's loneliness. These are things of the mind and it is here that people need to cure themselves. It depends on the mind and the heart, and on emotion and security, and by themselves these are powerless unless they're surrounded by real love. Yet people seem unable to hold onto this love—they have sold their hearts to a pile of materialistic baubles. People are frightened of silence, of surrender to God, of prayer. They search in the darkness, in a stupor. They don't feel at home anywhere. People are standing outside in the cold. And they can't offer security and hospitality to anyone else either.

A return to God, as towards a father who has written your name in the palm of his hand, may work wonders.

A friend

You can endure anything and live through anything
so long as a friend stands by you, even if he can do
nothing but say a few words or stretch out a hand.
A friend in your life is like bread and wine—a blessing.
A friend in your life is the most powerful comfort in
every need. A friend is true human goodness, in which
you sense a sign of godlike goodness. Believe me, the
clearest answer from a social worker, a psychiatrist or
an official, or the best-intentioned help from the
authorities, means less to a person in distress than a
simple gesture, a heart-felt word from a friend.
Last Sunday, why did that man on the telephone say,
"I am desperate. I don't want to live any more. I've
spent every last penny of my savings on a psychiatrist.
Fifty dollars a session. After that, to the doctor, then
the pharmacist for pills, and when they've gone I will be
back to square one again."
. . . And that woman last Thursday; "Say something.
I'll do something foolish. I've got four children. I've got
everything. But I'm tired of living."
Was there nobody who could have been a friend to
them, who could have offered them a little security in
this world, where everything is tottering about them?
Doctors, psychologists can't cope with it anymore.
People are victims of a contaminated mental
environment. Pills offer no solution. It has to do with
simple human kindness, so that each person can find a
cushion of security in another.

Comfort

Nobody can live without comfort.
But comfort is not like alcohol.
It's no injection,
no sleeping pill which merely numbs you,
and then plunges you into an even darker night.
Comfort is not a flood of words.
Comfort is a healing balm on a deep wound.
Comfort is a sudden oasis in an empty desert,
which makes you believe in life again.
Comfort is a soft hand on your forehead,
that makes you feel at peace.
Comfort is the gentle face of someone close to you
who understands your tears,
who listens to your troubled thoughts,
who sticks by you
through your doubts and anxieties,
and who shows you a few guiding stars
in the dark night.

Where you are always welcome

You can't live without somebody who likes you,
who thinks you're worthwhile,
who finds a place for you in his life,
someone whom you can occasionally turn to
—with total trust,
someone who cares about you,
and who always welcomes you.
You meet so many people in life,
but only a few special people come into your life,
and grow to be a part of your life,
become your 'family'.
I tell you, it is a great thing, a blessing,
if these are good people,
people who make you feel secure,
who, at heart, you feel at home with.
Can you imagine how horrible it must be,
if you never meet a single person in your whole life,
who spontaneously stretches out his arms to you.
Yet, today there are countless people
who have nobody anywhere,
nobody to care,
nobody who will put themselves out,
nobody who will give something of his heart.
And yet, these strangers also need so much,
their hearts also long
for a little sign of affection,
some warmth, some tenderness . . .
arms to run into, in a search for security.
Children especially, who are most often deprived of this,
are being marked for life, and later fill the homes,
the institutions and often the prisons.

Searching for security

Every person who comes into this world,
searches his whole life through for security.
He wants to find a home,
a little protection and human warmth.
A person who can't find security is a damaged person,
a failure, an unlucky person,
someone who doesn't feel at home in his own skin.
A child needs to find tender, soft security
with his father and mother.
Do you realise the tremendous responsibility
of two people who bring a child into the world?
A man seeks security with his wife and vice versa.
And people seek security from each other,
in marriage and in friendship.
The foundation of all security is *love*.
Selfishness and lack of love destroy all security,
and change a person into a homeless,
solitary damaged creature,
always agitated and never fulfilled.
The tragedy of our time
is that we can no longer give each other security.
We can't welcome each other, can't open our homes,
because we have forgotten about love,
because we have forgotten God,
the spring of all love.
We ourselves are no longer secure!

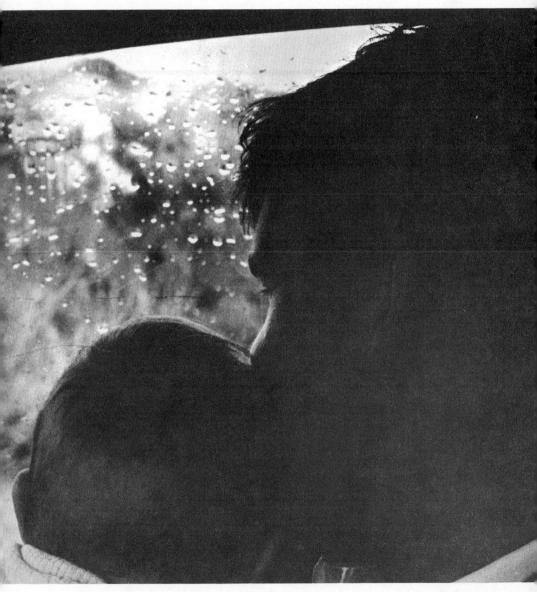

Recipe for sunshine

Accept each day as a gift, a joy.
Don't get up too late.
Look in the mirror
and grin at yourself.
Say "good morning" to yourself
to get in a little practice
for when you need to say it to others.

If you know the ingredients of sunshine,
you can make it just as easily
as today's soup.
Take a large portion of goodness.
Toss in big chunks of patience
—patience with yourself,
and patience with others.
Don't forget a pinch of humor
to help digest disappointments.
Mix with a big dollop of zest for work.
Cover with happy laughter
and there you have it
—the sunshine recipe of the day!

Love with a capital L

These days, who still knows what Love is?
Love, with a capital L?
Isn't the word Love horribly devalued
in ads and trashy newspapers and sex magazines,
where it is dirtied by the hands
of ruthless, faceless 'businessmen'?
Have their products of words and pictures
got anything at all to do with Love?
Are they turning our instruments of culture
into sewers for people
who never grew up beyond their waists?
And is their only aim to make big money?

These days, who still knows
that Love is about 'giving' and 'surrender',
about deep joy from 'giving oneself' to another,
in giving one's heart to another,
with tenderness, with gentleness,
with friendliness, with forgiveness, with peace,
with the surrender of might and ownership,
and with the surrender of physical power?

**These days, who still knows that Love
is about responsibility?**

We are completely dependent
on each other
for food, clothes,
housing, transport,
entertainment,
for anything that can be bought with money.
But we are even more dependent
on each other for our happiness.
And this can't be had for money.
The things of the heart—and love—
these are free.

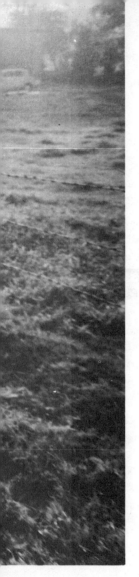

Love is like the sun

For a lot of people,
the sun is the most ordinary thing in the world.
Yet it works a wonder every day.
It lights up the world for me.
It fights against the clouds to see me
and to give me a beautiful day.
At night, it goes to the other side of the earth
to give its light to the people there.
If I snuff out the sun,
I am in the blackest darkness
and in the iciest cold.
That's what it's like with love.
If love rises in my life,
then it brings light and warmth.
If I have love,
I can do without many things.
But, if love goes down in my life,
the shadows grow even longer,
and I move quietly into the night and the cold.
Love is like the sun.
Anyone who has love can do without many things.
Anyone who lacks love, lacks everything.

A 'happiness' ticket?

Life is like a lottery.

Many people think they have drawn the wrong lot.
And what is still worse they are convinced that their
neighbor, who goes to a few more parties, has the best
ticket.

And yet, lottery tickets don't differ so very much. One
person may allow himself a few more 'frills' than
another, but that's all. The difference lies in the way of
looking at things, and in the way of accepting them.
And that depends on ourselves.

I have met a good many people, completely different
from each other. I have listened to their deepest secrets.
But never have I come across the person who had
drawn 'the' ticket—the big, beautiful, perfect,
happiness ticket.

Somewhere, sometime, they had all had their troubles.
The faithful call it a 'cross'. The non-believers say, "I
am unlucky".

Among them were gay, joyful people who kept going
through sorrow and great tragedy. Others were forced
down by strains and hardships; knocked down and
made bitter and rebellious. Often they both went
through identical problems, and yet the result was so
entirely different.

Yes, life *is* a lottery. But we ourselves can really do so
much about it!

Live today!
Love life today!
Be happy today!
Free your heart.
Don't let your delight in life
and your happiness
depend on a
hundred and one trivialities.

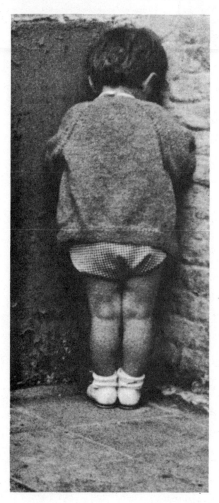

You must learn to fly blind from time to time,
like a pilot in fog.
You know what your tasks are each day.
Do them blindly.
Without thinking.
Without hesitation.
Give yourself up blindly
to someone else's leadership.
Have patience.
And have even more patience with yourself.

Right there

If I open every stop,
in an endless song of mourning,
I find myself only deeper in gloom.
Black thoughts
always bring new miseries down on my head.
I must live for today, bury the past.
I can't change it anyway.
All I can do
is to keep a window open
to all the beautiful memories,
and not worry too much about tomorrow.
What are my assets today?

> My health.
> The sun in the sky.
> Enough to eat and drink.
> A child who laughs with me.
> Flowers in my home.

Perhaps I am searching too far away for happiness?
It's like having a pair of glasses.
I don't see them,
when they're sitting on my nose.
Right there!

Every morning you must be grateful for the new day. Or are you afraid of life? Is it too heavy for you? Do you go to bed each night with a sigh of relief? "Thank God! Another day is over!" Perhaps you're bored stiff and everything seems senseless, useless. Possibly you are really too well off and your spirit is being stifled. Perhaps the four wheels of your car have become the most important parts of your body, and the TV has stolen your companionship. Possibly you continuously crave 'entertainment'. It never satisfies you. You are no longer human if, under the pressure of today's dominating mentality, you let yourself be reduced to a thing that produces, earns money and consumes. For you, flowers don't bloom any more. Children don't play any more. People don't laugh any more. You are dead, because you let love die in your heart. You look for happiness where you will never find it, in lifeless and senseless things which tempt you, but can never satisfy you. Wake up! Get up! Come alive! Tomorrow the sun will rise, and you won't notice it at all!

It all depends on your heart

You think more with your heart
than with your intellect.
You look with your heart at people and at things.
You see everything with your heart.
Your relationships with your neighbors
depend on your heart.
What your heart longs for, you will defend
with all your intelligence, with all your strength.
Your heart chooses the people
and the things you want to live for.
Your heart chooses the ideas,
the politics, the systems you want to fight for.
The heart darkens or lights up the reason.
The proper state of the heart is: love.
If your heart is full of selfishness and distrust
your heart will never find the way to peace.
This is, in fact, the only explanation for the fiasco
of all the round-table talks,
of these endless discussions about peace in the world.
The people don't like each other
and that is exactly why they will never be united.
The only thing they reach is a shaky balance of power,
based on mutual distrust.
Let them keep silent about peace
so long as it means nothing more
than those anxious, caged-in international meetings
held on the brink of a volcano,
or that tense co-existence
in the same country, even in the same house.
Peace, joy and happiness in the world
are not a matter for the intellect
but a thing of the heart.
Every society, whether it is called Christian,
socialist, communist or Maoist, is rotten to its core,
as long as the hearts of the people are not changed.
The first duty of every man is to look to his heart.

You spend hours cleaning your car.
You take all your time choosing your clothes.
You're not nervous sitting under the drier
having a hairdo.
Why do you spend so little time
looking after your heart?
If you live on the outside only,
always concerned about your outward appearance,
your make-up, your good name, your façade,
then your happiness hangs on the thread
of outward uncertainties.
Then you are happy today
and unhappy tomorrow,
in a good temper today
and miserable tomorrow.

Look inside yourself.
Do something about your inner self,
about the interior of your heart.
For your feelings and longings are found there,
and they either cause conflict
or fulfill you beyond measure.

Other people have to look at your face

Don't forget
that your face is really intended for others.
Other people have to look at it.
And nothing is quite so miserable and depressing
as having to look at an unfriendly, ugly face
for hours and days on end.
Your face is more than a pretty front,
more than a signboard, more than a visiting card.
Care for your face,
not only for yourself,
so that it's pleasant to look in a mirror,
but most of all for others.
Spreading various brands of beauty cream
on your forehead, nose and cheeks
is not the best kind of care.
Nor is plucking your eyebrows.
Nor is gluing on false eyelashes.
Nor is putting on eye shadow.
Take care of your face from the inside.
Put light and friendship in your eyes instead.
Relax your mouth. Let it smile.
Turn your face into a friendly face.
You can do this if you go a little deeper
and tidy up your heart.
Drag out of it all that brooding, criticism and worry
about things that have nothing to do
with making you happy.
Away too with that sad going-over
of your daily mistakes.
Put on your best, your most friendly,
your most pleasing face
and it won't be hard for people to like you.

People's faults

How do I see the faults of my husband,
my wife, my father and mother, my children?
The faults of my colleagues, my workmates,
my fellow students, my neighbors?
Don't get me wrong.
I don't mean the faults of people
I don't know personally,
nor faults which are no concern of mine,
nor those that don't hurt me.
I mean the failings and shortcomings
of the people right next to me,
people I'm supposed to love,
whom I live and work with every day.
If the faults of these people get on my nerves,
if I nag about them,
then I had better take a quick look at my heart.
For then love has become worn.
I should not be totally blind
about the failings of others.
But if I really love,
I wouldn't see so many flaws and faults.
Love is always a little bit blind.
But, if love and friendship weaken,
that sympathetic blindness is also lost.
The inevitable defects and faults of others
begin to put me on edge.
They become a burden.
They seem to grow bigger every day.
My eyes get worse,
and finally I see nothing but black.
Nothing but faults and failings. Ugly things.

**There are people
who give out light.
And there are people
who darken everything.**

Pessimism

You are not a pessimist if you grieve over a deep
wound in your heart or when a sea of problems weighs
you down. Neither are you a pessimist when you are
deeply saddened by the unbearable suffering of so
many innocent people. Nor because of the savage
violence and injustice in the world.

A pessimist is a person who spends a lifetime in a
darkroom — developing only negatives. A pessimist is a
person who says it's going to rain, when the sun is
shining. When things are going well, he says it won't
last. He's suspicious whenever anyone is kind or
friendly.

A pessimist has poor eyesight; he never sees the pretty
things.

A pessimist has poor hearing; he never hears the good
news.

He feels the pain but not the joy. For him everything is
dark, empty, sad. He never turns the coin over, to see
things from the other side.

**Medical diagnosis: "Pessimism has a
detrimental effect on digestion and blood
pressure."
Conclusion: "Optimists live longer than
pessimists."
Afterthought: "Pessimists don't live, they are
dead long before they are buried."**

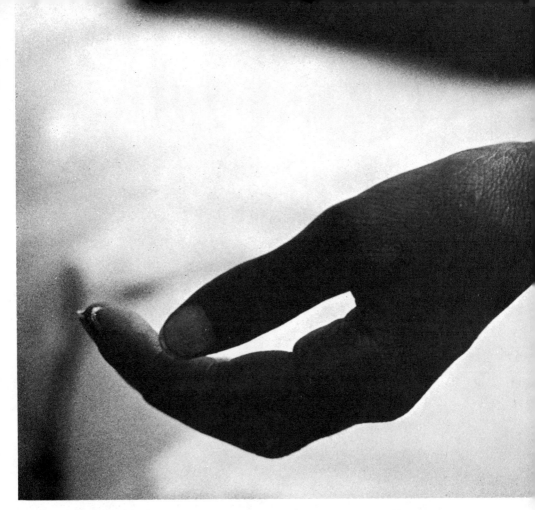

You would hate the rich

Being poor . . .
You don't know what it is.
Being poor
like *millions* of people in the poor countries.
You don't know what it is.
Demolish your house
and build a hovel of mud,
or corrugated iron or cardboard.
You can't have a bedroom
and certainly not a private study.
Replace your armchairs
with benches and boxes.

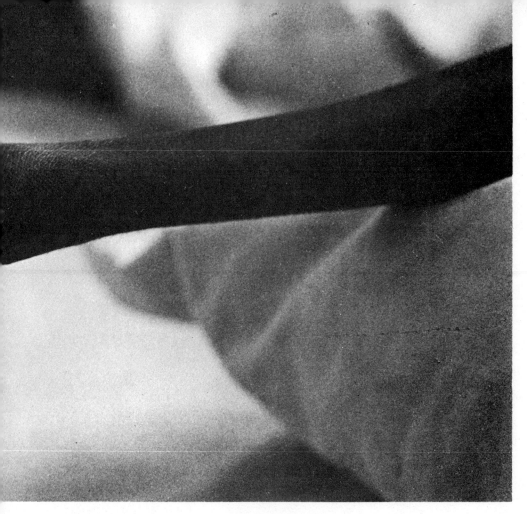

Away with your car, your TV, your radio.
Switch off the electricity, unplug the telephone.
Turn off the gas and the water supply.
Away with your newspapers, your stereo,
your refrigerator and your freezer.
Throw out your smart clothes.
If you're ill, there will be no druggist, no doctor
and no hospital.
If being poor is like that
could you then care
for those who have all these things in abundance
and would not share them?
You would grow to hate the rich.
I fear
that this is beginning to happen in many lands.

My house is your house

Try to like people.
Love everybody.
Above all that means to welcome every person
you meet on your way through life.
That means opening your heart,
your house, your possessions
in such a way that the other person
is never made to feel inferior,
but can accept your kindness
as part of the way you are.
Nothing must be forced.
Everything should be spontaneous.
Hospitality is not something that is learned.
You won't ever find it in a book.
It is a deep inward attitude
of openness and communicativeness.
It belongs to the mystery of being a real person.

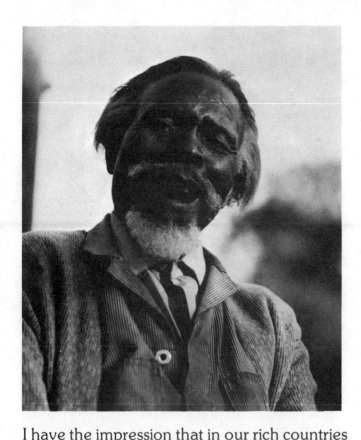

I have the impression that in our rich countries
we have lost our ability to welcome people.
Yet, hospitality is one of the highest human values.
We must go to the poor to rediscover real hospitality.
The poor man in Africa, for example,
invites you to his miserable little hut
—built from mud, from corrugated iron or cardboard
and keeps repeating, "My house is your house!
You *must* come and have a cup of tea.
You *must* come and have something to eat."
And when evening falls, he won't let you go.
You must sleep there.
He will unroll his best mats for you,
and God only knows where he himself is going to sleep.
And if such a poor person comes to our rich land?
He may *never ever* be invited into a home
—not even for a cup of tea!

Children have to be very patient with grown-ups

Do you ever get the feeling that children are puzzled about the dull narrow-mindedness of grown-ups? When grown-ups are together they talk in code. When they meet somebody they ask about his job, his possessions, his connections and his education. If they talk about a house they say, "It costs one hundred thousand dollars". And in their head it's already there.

They don't need to know anything else. They know
precisely what a $100,000 house is.

But if you tell children about a friend they ask, "Does
he collect butterflies? Can he whistle? Can he play
snap? Can we go swimming?"

If you speak about a house they'll ask about its color,
the kind of garden, whether the lawn's big enough to
play on. They will ask "Is there an attic? Have they got
a canary?"

Anything children touch is suddenly fresh and natural,
full of color and warmth. Grown-ups don't
understand it at all. They are that way. They talk about
making a living and worry continuously about money.
And that is why children have to be so patient with
grown-ups.

I am convinced that what happens in our schools and universities is much more important and more decisive for the future than all the activities in our factories, workshops and offices.

There, people are being formed—or deformed.

If their only concern is about intellectual development, about cramming brains full of facts, they will produce perfect robots, but not men. The schools and universities where professors and teachers are only paid to churn out knowledge and specialization lay the foundations for a spiritually bankrupt community. Education does not consist of developing the intellect only, but in forming the total person, including his heart and character. Education is the passing down, from generation to generation, of the spiritual values which give meaning and substance to life. That passing down is not by word alone but more by making those words alive and visible in your own way of life. Education is a shared mission for parents, schools, universities, the press, radio, television and advertisers. A heavy responsibility.

Two ways to live

You learn to drive a car.
You dress fashionably.
You learn languages.
You feel at home with technical things.
You learn a whole heap of things.
Despite that, one day you find yourself in a corner
You learned everything,
except how to live.
They said to you;
get on in life, make yourself a career, earn money
take advantage of events, acquire lots of things
—as if happiness sat next to greed.
People are jackals in a vast jungle,
they hunt for bread and amusement.
They think they are free.
But they are chained
to their own senseless desires.

There are two ways to live.
One begins with restraint
and ends in fulfilment.
The other starts with a lust for pleasure
and ends in dissatisfaction, weariness of life,
disappointment and every kind of neurosis.

**If you have time for someone,
don't keep looking at your watch.**

You are a lovely person. Yet you already carry your
entire past on your back and you also want to burden
yourself with your entire future.
That is far too much for you.
Your life is given to you in slices of twenty-four hours.
So why do you want to carry it all at once? You weren't
meant for that.
That could *kill* you!

Look for the person behind each face

When you deal with objects you can ignore love.
You can cut down a tree, pull out a bush.
You can throw down a glass, knock over a chair,
or fling a shoe into the corner.
When you handle objects you can ignore all kinds of things—
though it hurts when you see somebody trample on a flower.
But in dealing with people you have to care for them.
And if you can't love people, stay in your little corner.
Keep yourself busy or occupy yourself
with dumb lifeless things.
But leave people alone.

Perhaps you're too involved with administration
and you only see papers and formulas and numbers
and never suspect a human face behind them.
Or perhaps you're involved in your work
and when you open your mouth to your juniors or workmates,
a sort of bark comes out.
Or you're so busy at your office, school, or shop
that you go through whole days
without meeting a single person—just talking dolls.

Look for the person behind each face.
Like people. Like the small ones, big ones,
pretty ones, ugly ones, happy ones, grumpy ones,
handy ones, clumsy ones,
the successful ones and the failures.
Your love will do them good.
You yourself know immediately
when someone is interested in you,
when someone likes you or not.
If someone cares for you, if he feels friendly,
then everything seems different, each moment wonderful.
The same goes for others when you make contact with them.

Be gentle

Living together is difficult.
Our words are often charged with threats and violence.
Protests. Contests. Confrontations.
What for? To achieve a better, more humane society?
By the very loss of respect
and all gentleness in our human relations,
we are making our society even less humane.
We always keep believing in power.
We always want to be in the right
and try, by every possible means, to come out on top.
Our emotional life has become shriveled, poor.
More than ever we need gentleness and tenderness.
If only you knew how vulnerable all things are,
and how lonely people are,
you would be gentle.
Think of the many, many people

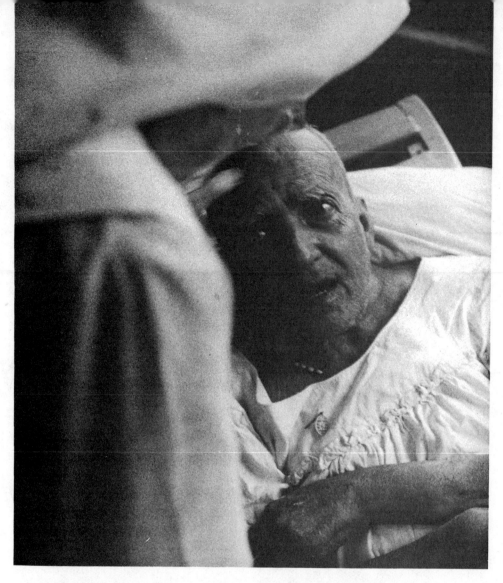

who are pushed out of the mainstream of life—
through sickness, need, bad luck or poverty.
They long for a smile, wait for a kind word,
look for friendship and understanding.
Think of the sick, the old, the disabled,
who seldom, if ever, feel a warm hand,
who never enjoy the warmth
of someone's arms around them,
who are buried in their own isolation.
Be utterly tender and gentle to all people around you
and never leave anyone out in the cold.

Nothing can weigh you down as much as your inability to forgive. And nothing is quite so tragic as to live day after day, with a sharp stone of resentment and hate in your heart.

Oh yes, I can understand it.

Somebody, perhaps many people, have done you wrong and little by little your heart has become cold. You are not the same person any more. That surprises you. You're no longer so soft, so gentle, so good. Your affection has turned cold, your sympathy turned to aversion. Where once there was a bond, there is now a break. It hurts. Friendship has turned to aggression. Your love has slowly turned to hate. It makes you miserable; you feel trapped. Your shutters are down and the sun can't shine through. Life weighs you down. Deep down in your heart you long to be free.

But there is only one way, believe me.

Forgiveness!

Forgive. I know just how hard that is, but it's worth it. Forgiving is a kind of creativity. It brings new life, new joy. It creates new possibilities within yourself and within others.

You have to forgive again and again. You must forgive seventy times seven times. Forever. Because you, too, need so much forgiveness.

*A kind of
creativity*

Growing old is an art

You are going to grow very old, if there is no fatal accident, no heart-failure or serious illness on your agenda. But what pleasure is there in old age if it brings with it all the plagues of Egypt—stiff legs, rheumatism, arteriosclerosis, memory loss, failing hearing, weak eyes, isolation and loneliness?

Machines that don't work any more go on the scrap-heap. Can people stay human and happy if they aren't able to take part in the productive process?

This depends on your whole environment; your family, relations and friends. It depends on the standard of care provided for older people and on a decent retirement pension. But mostly, it depends on you.

You must learn how to grow old.

Growing old is no disaster. Your old age doesn't have to be a period of misery. Learn to grow old with a young heart.

It is an art in itself.

Accept life

To enjoy a little happiness, to have a taste of heaven on earth, you must accept life, your own life, just as it is now. You must be at peace with your work, with the people around you, with their faults and their imperfections. You must be content with your husband, your wife, even if you now realize you did not marry the ideal husband or the ideal wife. (I don't believe they exist anyway.) You must be at peace with the size of your purse, your status in the community, with your face (which you did not choose yourself), with your home, your furniture, your clothes, with your own living standards—even if your neighbor's things are so much better and so much finer, so you think. Accept life. You only have one skin. You can't be born again in another one.

We need to be understood

In a moment of depression, of weakness or anxiety in your life, it is of overwhelming importance that you come across a good person, someone with understanding who doesn't give you an ice-cold lecture but consoles you and supports you.

We are poor, weak people. None of us are angelic beings complete with halo and wings. None of us can walk in clouds of perfection.

We all need understanding, sympathy and forgiveness. And this is the gift we can offer to each other in the name of Jesus of Nazareth.

Do you know him? Many know him by name. Few know him as a friend. He wants to free men from wrong. And the greatest wrong is lovelessness. He liked poor people and sinners and was only angered by rich people and hypocrites—people who thought they were so perfect they didn't need forgiveness.

"Whichever one of you has committed no sin, may throw the first stone at her," he said.

And he told of the prodigal who returned and was welcomed without reproach, with open arms and no question as to how or why. On the contrary. Jesus is not like a person. He is love. He holds a welcoming feast for every prodigal son and offers paradise to a a repentant murderer. He writes in the sand for the faithless wife. He tenderly carries the lost sheep on his shoulder. And once he told us the one single thing we should know about him: "Learn from me for I am gentle and humble in spirit."

I love this Jesus more than I can say. He lives for me. I would so like you to know him, not as someone from the past, but as a living friend, beside you.

Run to the woods!

Foot down on the accelerator and just driving on? Oh, come on. Stop and get out. Run to the woods!
Hours on end behind a drink in a smoke-filled bar, drowned by deafening canned music? Oh please, come outside before you wilt and go moldy. Run to the woods!
A diary crammed with appointments and dashing from one meeting to another? Run to the woods!
Tired of life and shut up in your own little world of exaggerated, useless things? Run to the woods!
There stand the trees, just waiting for you. The heavenly trees, silently enjoying the stillness and the spring sap rising to the very tops of their branches. There are the birds, just waiting to sing for you. Where are you, people, to listen? Rest, quietness and indescribable peace are waiting for you there.
You want to live fully. But living fully does not mean living frenziedly, running day-in, day-out, under the pressure of a hundred-and-one little emergencies. You want to know it all, to be part of it all, to digest it all. To get ulcers from it too?
Run to the woods! Take a packed lunch and thermos. Lie down at the foot of a tree, a blade of grass between your teeth and simply delight in doing nothing. Then, the best ideas will come to you out of the blue. And the most beautiful dreams. Then all those weighty indoor problems will simply disappear.
Run to the woods! There you'll find a clear mind, a calm soul and a peaceful heart.
And I can hear you saying to me, "If only I could."
And I will answer, "You're already on your way!"

When you're tired,
when everything's against you,
when you don't know where to turn
and you feel really wretched,
think of the beautiful days,
days when you were friendly with everyone
like a carefree child.

Don't forget the beautiful days,
during times when the horizon, as far as the eye can see,
is dark, without a ray of light,
when your heart is heavy,
and perhaps filled with bitterness,
when all hope of renewed joy and happiness
seems to have evaporated.

Don't forget the beautiful days

Then, I beg you,
search carefully through your memories
for those beautiful days,
the days when everything was so good,
with not a cloud in the sky,
when there was someone close to you,
when you felt so warm towards someone
who by now has perhaps disillusioned or deceived you.

Don't forget the beautiful days.
If you do forget them, they will never return.
Fill your mind with joyful thoughts.
Fill your heart with forgiveness, tenderness and love.
Fill your home with laughter
and everything will go well again.

121

"Mankind,
I love
you"

That's a strange but happy message.
Or is it only an illusion, a dream?

I believe in a new beginning for the whole world,
when every soldier, wherever his war,
will throw his gun to the ground
and will call out to his enemy, seen or unseen:
"Friends, I love you.
I can't kill you. I won't do you any harm."

I believe in a world of new opportunities
when the rich, ashamed of their wealth
will give up their power and possessions
and will go to the poor, saying:
"Friends, I love you.
Forgive me, I took too much for myself.
I will sit at your table to share bread
and to share the flowers of peace in the sun."

I believe in the miracle
when, in every house,
in every street, in every city,
people will say to their neighbors:
"My friends, my brothers, I love you.
I'll never say bitter things again.
I'll fill my heart with caring.
I'll fill my hands with the gifts of friendship."

"Friends, mankind, I love you."
Speak out. Convey it.
With or without words.
Say it with a smile, with a gesture of reconciliation,
with a handshake, with a word of thanks,
with a touch on the shoulder, with a spontaneous hug,
with a kiss, with a twinkle in your eye.
Make it known in a thousand little ways. Fresh every day.
"Mankind, I love you."

CHRISTIAN HERALD ASSOCIATION AND ITS MINISTRIES

CHRISTIAN HERALD ASSOCIATION, founded in 1878, publishes The Christian Herald Magazine, one of the leading interdenominational religious monthlies in America. Through its wide circulation, it brings inspiring articles and the latest news of religious developments to many families. From the magazine's pages came the initiative for CHRISTIAN HERALD CHILDREN'S HOME and THE BOWERY MISSION, two individually supported not-for-profit corporations.

CHRISTIAN HERALD CHILDREN'S HOME, established in 1894, is the name for a unique and dynamic ministry to disadvantaged children, offering hope and opportunities which would not otherwise be available for reasons of poverty and neglect. The goal is to develop each child's potential and to demonstrate Christian compassion and understanding to children in need.

Mont Lawn is a permanent camp located in Bushkill, Pennsylvania. It is the focal point of a ministry which provides a healthful "vacation with a purpose" to children who without it would be confined to the streets of the city. Up to 1000 children between the ages of 7 and 11 come to Mont Lawn each year.

Christian Herald Children's Home maintains year-round contact with children by means of an *In-City Youth Ministry*. Central to its philosophy is the belief that only through sustained relationships and demonstrated concern can individual lives be truly enriched. Special emphasis is on individual guidance, spiritual and family counseling and tutoring. This follow-up ministry to inner-city children culminates for many in financial assistance toward higher education and career counseling.

THE BOWERY MISSION, located at 227 Bowery, New York City, has since 1879 been reaching out to the lost men on the Bowery, offering them what could be their last chance to rebuild their lives. Every man is fed, clothed and ministered to. Countless numbers have entered the 90-day residential rehabilitation program at the Bowery Mission. A concentrated ministry of counseling, medical care, nutrition therapy, Bible study and Gospel services awakens a man to spiritual renewal within himself.

These ministries are supported solely by the voluntary contributions of individuals and by legacies and bequests. Contributions are tax deductible. Checks should be made out either to CHRISTIAN HERALD CHILDREN'S HOME or to THE BOWERY MISSION.

Administrative Office: 40 Overlook Drive, Chappaqua, New York 10514
Telephone: (914) 769-9000